Why Wash?

LEARNING ABOUT PERSONAL HYGIENE

Written by Claire Llewellyn
and
illustrated by Mike Gordon

Some of us
always seem to
look nice! ...

and smell nice!

4

These people take care of themselves.
They're good to be around.

When you were a baby, your parents took care of you. They washed you, changed you and kept you clean.

You smelt gorgeous ...

... well, most of the time!

As you got older, you learned
how to take care of yourself.

And now you do most things
for yourself ...

... Don't you?

Some people don't like washing.
They can't see the point ...

10

... or they don't seem to have the time.

But think what would happen if
you stopped washing.

← Greasy hair

← mucky eyes
← waxy ears
← Bad breath
← Bad teeth
← Grubby neck

Tom →

Smelly feet!
←

What would your friends think then?

It's not hard to take care of yourself.
You just do a few things
every morning ...

WASHING YOUR FACE

CLEANING YOUR TEETH

BRUSHING YOUR HAIR

HAVING A BATH

... and a couple more every night.

CLEANING YOUR TEETH

Some things are tricky and need a helping hand.

But they only need doing once or twice a week.

Taking care of yourself makes you look good and feel good ...

Germs are tiny, invisible things that live all around us.

They are in the air ...

on things that we touch ...
and even on you and me.

Germs attack our bodies.
They rot our teeth ...

give us coughs and colds ...
and can make us feel very ill.

CLEAN
HANDS

Germs spread easily from
your hands and can make
you feel poorly.

GERMS FROM
THE CAT

GERMS ON
THE FINGERS

GERMS ON
THE CAKE

GERMS IN
THE MOUTH

GERMS IN
THE TUMMY

Germs make one person ill ...
and another ... and another.

23

We get rid of germs when we wash our hands.

We need to do this every time we go to the toilet, and before we touch any food.

Flies can be dirty and help to
spread nasty germs.

Try and keep food away
from flies.

25

Every time you cough or sneeze, germs
shoot out into the air ...

... and float around until other people breathe them in.

Always catch your germs in a handkerchief first.

No one likes feeling poorly. But if you are ill, nobody else wants your germs.

Keeping clean is a good way to
wash germs away and makes you
look wonderful, too.

TOPIC WEB

Maths
Calculate how much water a dripping tap loses in a day. Work out how many times you have a bath, wash your hands and brush your teeth in one week.

Design and Technology
Design some novelty products such as sponges and toothbrushes that would encourage children to enjoy washing and keeping clean.

History
Find out about objects that were used for keeping clean in the past. Ask grandparents about their hygiene routines when they were children. What facilities did they have in the home?

Science
Work out some ways you can stop germs spreading at school; perhaps in the kitchens or toilets.
Find out how to keep different sorts of pets clean.

Geography
Find out about the supply of fresh water in different countries of the world.

Why Wash?

R.E.
Find out about the religious significance of washing rituals in different religions.

Language
Compile a list of words to do with health and hygiene, and terms related to health and germs.
Compose poems about being clean and being dirty.

Art and Craft
Make a poster to encourage children to wash and enjoy being clean, and showing the problems caused by not doing so.

Music
Use different percussion instruments to imitate the sounds of running water, of someone scrubbing and brushing teeth.

P.E./Dance/Drama
Check the facilities at school for washing after sport.
Discuss how it could be made easier for children to wash properly after P.E. or dance lessons.

GLOSSARY

germs Tiny forms of animal or plant life – some which cause illnesses.

invisible Something that cannot be seen with your eyes, unless viewed under the microscope.

BOOKS TO READ

Bathtime by Gill Tanner and Tim Wood (History Mysteries series, A & C Black)

This book looks at familiar objects in the bathroom and how they have changed over the years.

Loos Through the Ages by Richard Wood (Rooms Through the Ages series, Wayland, 1998)

This book follows the changing style of toilets through the ages.

My Amazing Body: A First Look at Health and Fitness by Pat Thomas (Wayland, 2002)

This book shows children how to care for their bodies to keep them clean, fit and healthy.

INDEX

bath 9, 15
body 21

care 5, 6, 8, 14, 18
clean 6, 29

ears 13

face 14
fingers 22
flies 25
food 24, 25
friends 13

germs 18, 19, 20, 21,
   22, 23, 24, 25, 26, 27,
   28, 29

hair 14
hands 22, 24

illnesses 21, 23, 28

morning 14
mouth 23

night 15

smell 4, 7

teeth 13, 14, 15, 21
time 11
toilet 24